BAD IDEAS

CALGARY PUBLIC LIBRARY

DEC   2018

BAD IDEAS

Michael V. Smith

NIGHTWOOD EDITIONS

2017

Copyright © Michael V. Smith, 2017

All rights reserved. No part of this publication may be reproduced,
stored in a retrieval system or transmitted, in any form or by any means,
without prior permission of the publisher or, in the case of photocopying
or other reprographic copying, a licence from Access Copyright,
the Canadian Copyright Licensing Agency, www.accesscopyright.ca,
info@accesscopyright.ca.

Nightwood Editions
P.O. Box 1779
Gibsons, BC V0N 1V0
Canada
www.nightwoodeditions.com

Cover image: Michael Caines
Cover design: Angela Yen
Typesetting: Carleton Wilson

Canada

 Canada Council   Conseil des Arts    BRITISH COLUMBIA
for the Arts   du Canada   ARTS COUNCIL
                                            An agency of the Province of British Columbia

Nightwood Editions acknowledges financial support from
the Government of Canada through the Canada Book Fund and
the Canada Council for the Arts, and from the Province of
British Columbia through the British Columbia Arts Council
and the Book Publisher's Tax Credit.

This book has been produced on 100% post-consumer recycled,
ancient-forest-free paper, processed chlorine-free
and printed with vegetable-based dyes.

Printed and bound in Canada.

CIP data available from Library and Archives Canada.

ISBN 978-0-88971-326-0

This is a book of anxieties, you might say, an address

to better understand them, an articulated relief.

It's dedicated to a few who have been a balm or a cure:

my mother and sister, who have loved me longer than anyone,

my grade ten high school English teacher Elaine MacDonald,

who read my first poems and very likely saved my life,

and my husband, Francis, who illuminates the corners.

CONTENTS

PRAYERS

Prayer for Irony   13
Prayer for Hatred   15
Prayer for Envy   16
Prayer for Paternal Love   18
Prayer for Happiness   20
Prayer for a Wig   21
Prayer for Promiscuity   22
Prayer for Humility   24
Prayer for Optimism   25
Prayer for Gender   26

DREAMS OF FRIENDS AND FAMILY

I Dream of Good Management   29
I Dream of the Accidental   30
I Dream the Inevitable   32
I Dream a Dated War Movie   33
I Dream of Creative Solutions   34
I Dream of Failed Attempts   36
I Dream the Future is Not Bright   38
I Dream of Things to Come   39
I Dream of Escape   40
I Dream of Fraternity   43
I Dream of Inadequacy   44
I Dream a Queer Allegory   46
A Woman Dreams the Birth of her Son   48
I Dream of a Bitter Mediocrity   50

QUEER

Awkward Moments   53

John Kissick's Painting   54

Handy Tips to Limit a Queer's Chances
of Being Gunned-Down   56

Advice for Every Moment of Change   60

Your Peers Die Like This   62

Letter, 10:28 pm   63

Family Friend   64

The Summer   65

Wolf Lake   68

A New Song   70

LITTLE THINGS

A Little Porno Story   75

A Little Story of a Bad Idea   76

A Little Story of the Burden in the World   79

A Little Rant for Whining   82

A Little Story of Dissociation   84

A Little Story of Solace   86

A Little Song to Make Sense of the World   88

Notes   91

Acknowledgements   93

About the Author   95

...in poetry there is no one behind the language being prayed to. It is the language itself which has to hear and acknowledge.

—John Berger, *And Our Faces, My Heart, Brief as Photos*

PRAYERS

Prayer for Irony

After his wife left him for a juggler
they met in the supermarket—a tall

reedy man with fingers too fine
for his short, plump torso—the artist

did what he'd always wanted and
bought a young terrier at the pound.

He named it Irony, a cleverness
in the face of grief, because wasn't it

he that suggested they invite his future
cuckold, the juggler, for coffee?

Around the house the dog pissed
everywhere paper hadn't been laid,

making damp the hall closet, the sofa
and bed. Irony was a model pup

when the artist was free and the holiest
hell at deadlines. If the man had baggies

the shit was diarrhetic. Each evening
the artist cried, the puppy padded

across the room and slept. When, after
weeks of being single, the artist said *yes*

to an invitation to picnic in the park
with that intern who held the elevator

on occasion just for him, of course
he brought Irony who vomited

grass on the girl's light blue Mary Janes.
Finally, the artist thought himself savvy

to rename the beast Happy. All day
the terrier bawled for the moon in

his small, convincing yowl until
the sun rose on the seventh day

and the man tried again with Lucky.
By noon, a transport had flattened fur

to grille, the nimble way a round dull
period at the end of a sentence

can render a trumped-up thought
finite.

Prayer for Hatred

Would evolution have given feathers
to the reptiles had they loved
the risks on the ground?

You resent your limitations, hatred
being the best of them. A force
for undoing, unavoidable,

hatred is your beast rising up
in the face of that which stands
between you and fresh water.

Must we debate if love
is its bright twin, or if love, siametic,
could live on its own?

Has hatred not liberated
more people than those who have done
the enslaving?

Dear hatred, sweet hatred,
do you not move our enemies
to know us better?

Prayer for Envy

Canvas envies paint.

The bullhorn envies
          the voice without need
of a battery.
          The diamond envies our indifference for coal.

Pavement envies the boot, whereas
          the stiletto envies grass

which is more true than
          the stiletto envies the boot

or that pavement
          could envy grass.

The needle envies
          the wound it closes, the scalpel
envies skin.

          The ground the air
for how it moves; the Earth
          its steady orbit.

The dead envy the living,
          above all, for their smell.
          Envy
envies only itself.

In a song, all silence is envied by its notes.
Notes being nothing
     but noise without a pause.

The hand
     envies the hangnail
which harms
     without intent.

Prayer for Paternal Love

All eight fingers on his right hand refuse
to be a blessing

so that even at the dinner table
he cannot pinch salt from the crowding
of his digits.

Days after he was born,
Only dogs,
his father had said,
could ignore them.

Eight splayed fingers on the back
yard stump, knuckles
around the wrist,
Hold still, his dad says.

The boy prays the octopus
of his hand contains
a secret.

Bouyancy

like silt that can storm
then settle, given time.

He has loved his father
less than either of them
would wish.

Now give it here,
his father says, and the boy
                    to prove the point
        reaches for their axe.

Prayer for Happiness

When your father dies and leaves you
more money than you anticipated
can you admit there is not in his death
some fickle breeze of how easy it is
to embrace happiness?

                Liquid,
hard to hold, happiness is an acid
not long contained, it leaks
through any trap. Assumes
any shape:

       Happiness comes to the hand
holding the knife that slits the throat.
Happiness in the eye of the kiddie
porn find online.

Relief is bedfellows with happiness
when the car crash fells someone
else's daughter, when cancer
takes down a killer who we breezily
forget is loved by family.

Each time we celebrate
the downfall of a dictator
we drag happiness through our muck
by its collar so that happiness
will not recognize itself.

Prayer for a Wig

in memory of Elise Partridge

In the untidy storage room before a reading,
she touched a small hand to her cancer wig with a laugh

at its benefits. Like, *my hair is always done;*
no more expensive cuts!

The irony had an echo, how the more
people you love the more bad news is had.

She smiled. We smiled. I described a drag mullet—
a dear friend's wig re-gifted, that she'd been given

with cancer at sixteen (what luck to be born
to outlive experimental treatments)

—that I admitted was a joy to wear. Proof
my dear friend lived.

Prayer for Promiscuity

Midnight in Stanley Park,
the moon is an ally. Night
breathes a chill into firs.

Men double as tree trunks,
appear a darker dark.

Within, your ears are readied eyes,
sift animal sounds from human,
some differences of intent.

The dark will always see better.
As though it hides our lovers

like the dead, dead before we met,
the night teaches us to miss
what we never had.

Across Lost Lagoon, the apartment
complexes rise, pixelated

a horizon lonelier than childhood.
If we'd been children together, perhaps
we could have saved each other.

When they lift from the shadows of trees
what do your palms reach for?

Have you noticed your fingertips,
bark peppering the skin? I could lick them
clean as silence if they rested here
and here awhile.

Prayer for Humility

Here is my father's leg
in the incinerator, freed
from the routine of glass
sharps, his poor sad dick
cathetered when Carmen,
the Phillipina nurse without
a wedding ring, arrives
for wound care.

Prayer for Optimism

my
nails mooned
with filth the
last three men salting
my breath I walk further
the woods dark & owning a
power I don't trust the alchemical dark
transforms us men young handsome as dreams scrubbed
clean by moonlight we are sick with some kind
of optimism every man potential nails mooned with filth four
men salting my breath I walk further the dark woods owning

Prayer for Gender

A teacher instructs the students
to draw their future selves.

One child draws the outline of a body
he is not going to be.

Watch how easily his hand transforms
the page. A dress where there was no dress.
Heels where none had been before.

He senses the future is something more
than black ink, white paper.

He draws another line, marking time.

DREAMS OF FRIENDS AND FAMILY

I Dream of Good Management

I'm emceeing a concert inside
a 24-hour supermarket. Children are
crushing potato chips into their mouths
as I announce the throat-singers. In aisle 15
a boy restacks small red potatoes.

I have to include grapes in my credits.
My superior is standing beside me
hissing into my ear what I should say next.
In annoyance and fear, I hold tight
the microphone. One of my co-workers,
the stupid boy who lives next door
but has beautiful lips, punctures
a milk carton and puts it back on the shelf.

I practice writing Ys with a marker
on a white board. Somehow, this
will make everything better.

I Dream of the Accidental

Walking the winter forest
      on a wide trail with three people.
          The ground muzzled
               in dense snow.

We come across a large hole
      many feet wide and ten feet deep, made
          by the death of my father.

I warn people not to fall in,
      only I find myself sinking
          through fresh powdery snow
     like quicksand. Whose death
is this, I wonder?

I am deep, feet down,
      facing my friends. Every attempt
          at release drops me further.

Two friends get help, one stays
      to be with me. It's a long wait.
          We watch a Seinfeld rerun
     on a TV suspended in the air above us
by a metal arm. George can't find
      his shoes. I know the routine,
          I've seen this episode.

Eventually, with accidental movement
       I fall deeper and pop out
            a hidden chute.
Saved, I ascend
       the small hill where
            I'd originally been.

My friends have returned with a young woman
       in a white uniform. Park staff.

She yells. We've called them
       for no reason and doesn't care
            when I try to explain
       how you can escape a hole
someone makes when they die.

I Dream the Inevitable

I'm in a chapel on the Titanic but
it's modern and kind of tacky.
The ceilings are twenty feet high.
Huge dark panels on the walls

where stained glass windows should be.
Walking past them, you see three-
dimensional representations
of the saints.

I remember a wine-coloured robe.
The framing on the panels is faux
gold metal.
I'm having sex with a guy. Heavy.

Black hair. Blunt nose. Acne
scars on his face. I think
he's hot and he's going to fuck me.
I have an image of my asshole.

I want him to use a condom. I won't let him
fuck me without a condom even tho
we're on the *Titanic* & I know exactly
what's going to happen.

I Dream a Dated War Movie

I'm watching a convoy of terrorists dressing up
their army vehicles as farm equipment and ramshackle carts.
They start down a road. They drive past a gang:
kids in hoodies, having a barbecue without suspicion.
In some 60s war movie montage, *A Bridge Too Far* or *Day into
    Night*,
the trucks shed their disguises, greying boards shattering onto
    pavement
revealing howitzers on trailers, tanks, jeeps. It's cut to music
just like a movie, a camera POV follows at highway speed.
One vehicle is a little shack, the size of an upright piano
which clatters away to reveal a white guy sitting at a desk,
    zooming
along the highway. He must be the leader.
                                        Jump-cut:
the scene is a living room with an elderly queer couple inviting
    me in.
Their place is decorated with doilies under everything, portraits
against wallpaper, rose furniture. I look out the door, to a small
suburban community. I know this is where the white terrorists
    attack.
I'm watching the movie, but the me in the room doesn't know,
just keeps coming in for dinner.

I Dream of Creative Solutions

A woman had two baby girls.
                In one version, they were twins. In
another, they were born a month apart.
                At any rate, both babies died.

The woman called Alastair,
                her member of parliament
for creative burial options.

                In the end, they wanted her babies
eaten in some way. She went to Alastair's
                to talk about their plan.
The door was unlocked; she let herself in.

                On a table were two glasses half-filled
with some sort of drink. It was then
                she realized she wanted to blend
her babies into a milkshake.

                Luckily, she knew where the ingredients
were kept in the apartment. In no time at all,
                she had two beautiful shakes.

They were cold and white, so white
                they were blue. They had
little dark brown flecks, the kind you see
                in eggnog.

As soon as she'd made her babyshakes,
                Alastair came home. There was an uproar.

Things become hazy. Somewhere,
               there is an open sky filled with dark, rolling
               clouds.
Somewhere, there is a burial of milkshakes.

               Somewhere, there is disgust, horror, and not
a small amount of admiration for the skillful
               blending of two babies into two glasses of
cool, pristine drinks.

I Dream of Failed Attempts

At the end of the night, a mouse
is trapped inside a plastic bag.

I delight in poking him through the plastic
until he bites my finger.

The puncture is deep.
I think, *This is probably*

a very bad thing, to have been bitten
by a mouse.

Without telling anyone, I find the antiseptic
in the bathroom

of my grandmother's bedroom.
There's a large dispenser on the table.

The room is dark,
like it so often was.

I treat my hand. I write
my cousin Jonathan in Paris,

over the internet. We compare tattoos
that neither of us has.

His is computer code.
I was bitten, I say

by a mouse.
This whole time, he replies,

I thought you were writing
because you missed me.

I Dream the Future is Not Bright

I'm hanging out with a trans guy
                underneath a bridge. It's summer.

                   SFR comes along and tells me
              she's going to art college at Dalhousie.

I tell her that she won't like
                       all the middle-class Jews there,
and some dude hanging around
            who doesn't care how thoroughly
                              I am
a middle-class Jew
attempts
            a conversation with me
          regarding anti-Semitism on the Left.

I Dream of Things to Come

I dream a boy about eight years old. He has
one runny, weepy eye.
I talk to a blonde woman, who goes, *Oh
that's the frank sign*, and lets me know
I can't ignore the frank sign.
She's a social worker or something.
She has blunt, straight hair shot with grey.
Jeans, a wide ass. A charcoal stretch top
with jet beading, like a drag queen.
She says when kids are abused or neglected
there is often a frank sign which, despite its
obviousness, people often ignore.

We both know this kid is being abused.
She descends the stairs as she tells me this.

I Dream of Escape

I'm walking down a wide city street,
                Main below Kingsway. It's twilight.
Danger in the air. Everybody
knows of some recent violence.

                Outside an auto repair shop with
           its blue and white storefront,
I hear rhythmic clanging—
renegade, youthful energy.
                Uh oh.
This is bad, I think, but
                keep walking.

I transform into a monk
        in burgundy and gold robes. I think
            this will protect me, but it doesn't.
        Men drag me in anyway.
(It's always men. Men
        in men stories
            doing men things.)

They have seized me
        because I'm a homo. A number of us
        sit inside the garage
        in a quiet line.

We too are all men.

        We're still.

The guys
      I thought mechanics
                are soldiers.
They're wearing desert camouflage, like Canadian
troupes in Afghanistan.

      The guy talking has a sweet face,
strawberry blond brush cut,
                creamy skin, rosy cheeks.
He informs us they will torture
and murder us then show
the videotapes on television.
      I will myself out of there.
      Somehow.

I flee through the city
      trying to get beyond their territory.

I transform.

      I am a woman and her husband.
We are pretending to be Polish refugees
because this will help.
          As a man
      I am wearing a not-very-good blue suit.
Me-as-wife is wearing a babushka.

Our ruse is working. But we have talked
      to a group of older men, casually,
sitting in a park, without realizing
they are powerful.

As we are leaving, one of them
                        —chunky, white-haired—
says he's from Germany. He's known Poles
and they didn't sound like us.

I Dream of Fraternity

I'm in a motel room with my brother.
   We're soldiers in the American Civil War
     and we're young men.

    He invites me
  to his side of the twilit room
to colour.

I use a dry felt pen on the trousers
   of a fat, English lord. I colour them
     aquamarine, the colour of innocence.

My brother touches my back with his hand.
   I can't believe my luck. My back feels
     alive, revived. He kisses me. I feel how
  tragic it is we will die young, although
I'm aware all lives are short.

I Dream of Inadequacy

I leave my parents' Colonial
Drive house

carrying small bowls
for a pair of neighbours,
one block north.

The light is grey, the only
strong source
from car headlights

that fade and divert themselves
away from me.

My movements slow,
treading molasses.

When I finally arrive
at the neighbours' home, my purpose
is lost.

       I peer in an open window
at piles of rubble.

There is a raven. Human-sized.
She informs me she's dead.

Another enters, says
we're all dead.

I tell her I'm alive, expecting
her to be as disgusted
by my life as I am.

She removes one bowl
from my hands, says,
Thank you.

That bowl is yours, she adds.
Or it will be.
                    And like that,
time speeds up again.

If you are *alive*, the raven says
as she turns to the rubble,
tell your relations
we have had enough.

I Dream a Queer Allegory

Check this. We're in a house
deep in the woods. I'm trying
to talk a committee-sized group—
maybe five—into having sex.
Nobody's going for it,
despite wild times before.

Maybe desire is dead?

A dark-haired stocky guy in a short-
sleeved cowboy shirt is talking
politics I admire. He's decided to be
at a particular place to protest American
policy when it's enacted. The actions
of a female, I think, like
Madeleine Albright.
                This guy
misuses the word *randomize*:
I randomized my choice of location.
I'm getting nowhere with the sex thing.

As I move my position to address
the group, I notice, speeding
between the trees, a grey car
—a huge, early model
American, a stripped-down '62
Pontiac my dad used to drive—
carrying a man to murder us.

I run to the woods. I know everyone else
will die. He's coming so fast.
The only thing I can imagine is to throw
my body to the floor of the woods, hoping
he won't notice me, and wait for night to fall.
Soon I will be a corpse.

A voiceover, like a horror
movie trailer, whispers:
                        Fog.
You seemed like a smart guy.
Fog. All alone in the woods.

A Woman Dreams the Birth of her Son

I dream the birth of my son.
There is no pain, only a pressure, and
a feeling of highness afterwards.
A feeling of being stoned.

The husband I do not have
asks me,

   How should we gender
the baby?

    We apparently left it
until now thinking
we would know the gender
by its face.

I am exhausted, barely present.
What do you think? I ask him.

    Ali Ubu, he says,
decidedly, and since
he strikes me as coherent
and rational in this moment, I agree.

We now have a tiny son gendered Ali Ubu.

In the weeks that follow, this
strikes me as ridiculous.
I can't even remember his gender.
Boob, I call this baby as a joke.

Ube, it says, mocking me
with its blank-slate perfection
and rounded lips. *Oob.*
Oob oob.
        I am convinced
I will love this child
one day or the next.

I Dream of a Bitter Mediocrity

People keep greeting me
to give me things I misplaced
at home or abroad. Some
travel a long way to do this.

It's like a project is suddenly
over and they're completing it
by turning in the items.

I'm happy to have my stuff back
but feel like with each sock
or badminton racket, my friends
are proving they're more
together than I am.

QUEER

Awkward Moments

I'm watching a videotape of my partner
and I making love at eighteen.

I can't get over how beautiful we were,
how thin and small our
waists and ribcages. How
much hair I had.

I found the tape in a box of things
at my mom's house; she'd obviously
been going through each
of my diaries and photos.

                    I thought you were happy,
and straight, my mom says that evening,
half-asleep, but bitterly.
                    I am happy, but I never
said I was straight, I tell her.

I pick up the box to take it with me.
You're welcome, she says as a gesture.

John Kissick's Painting

No. 5 doesn't know what it is.
        It will never be more
                than layered swathes
        of flesh-toned spillage, its
                intestinal grids
and blobs entwined

        in a frenzy of blue.
           Decades ago
        my mother locked my drunken
father out of the house.
        I was eleven. Dad

            knocked on the glass
        panes of the front door
at the base of the stairs
to our bedrooms, a call
        to my sister and I
           to undo the lock.

There was a stand-off
        and for whatever it might
           say about his children
he had to punch through
    a pane of glass
        to let himself in.

Need I say I dislike
          Kissick's painting. It has the same
messy rhythm as our dilemma
          on the stairs.
Its lines are too wholly
          human, nothing redemptive,

nothing of comfort except
          a kind of love like pity. A mess
                    on your porch, it can't
          help but make its panic
an offering.

Handy Tips to Limit a Queer's Chances of Being Gunned-Down

Strategy 1:

Stand in a group
on the street corner downtown
with a sign: *Gay Hugs.*

Give hugs.

Strategy 2:

Make more space
for outsiders more outside
than you.

Strategy 3:

Love our gay kids. Be kind-
ly queer to parents
in front of their children.

Strategy 4:

Organize more gay guerrilla
dance parties.

Strategy 5:

Don't call your queer history
anything other than trauma
when it is, in deed,
trauma.

Strategy 6:

Dismantle all systems
your privilege preserves.

Enfranchise your opposites. Don't share the fruit
of your tree but recognize the tree
is not owned at all.

Strategy 7:

Invite your straight allies
to speak up, call allies
to action, charge allies
to be allies.

Strategy 8:

Steal the guns
from your families' homes
while they're out.

Strategy 9:

Release queer events
to Muslim Black Latinx communities
any and all racialized minorities
because *#NotAllQueerPeople*
are white.

Strategy 10:

Fuck gender.

Strategy 11:

Hold people to a high standard
of character, not appearances.

Strategy 12:

Empower women. Listen
to them at work. Vote
them into office because
fewer women kill.

Strategy 13:

Listen. When haters speak,
that is our call to *listen*.
Not to their rhetoric, but
what lies behind it. What
unconscious fuel
is firing that engine.

Strategy 14:

Befriend conservatives
so you can babysit
their children.

Strategy 15:

Invite friends to make
more queer strategies.

Advice for Every Moment of Change

When you believe what
you believe and live the story

you tell yourself, then life does
what it does and changes

you will be as a character
dropped into the wrong setting.

You know the type, a brown guy
at the country club not

serving the food. A fag
recruited into major league

football. Any woman CEO
in the tech industry.

For a time, you may live happily
without drama.

In ignorance, it is easy
to believe no threat exists,

which is itself dramatic.
To forget is dramatic.

But take comfort that even
this clarity of ignorance

can be reduced to a scrawl;
a day's insights become

a poor simulacrum, a map
of elision and choice.

Frame your life as a fairy tale
buffer. Every word makes

a meeting place
between two false points.

Your Peers Die Like This

by complications
from HIV, overdose
brain tumour
bike accident

by dropping from a balcony
three stories (a second
fall making the first
suspicious)

cancer, days after
her birthday, by
choking, riding
in the bed
of a rolled pickup

asphyxiation
snorting Pam, by
infection from plastic
surgery

by heart attack moving
a buddy's sofa-bed

by aneurysm

by accident, of which
we do not speak

Letter, 10:28 pm

Clothed in bed. The day is pressed into my shirt.
Goats, gelato, beach, strawberries, popcorn.

So much indulgence I'd rather
have practised my French.

Step into my bedroom, a mess from being half-unpacked.
Remind me your lips are fresh with mischief.

Family Friend
for Asher

Joy! Skin-tingling joy, simple
as each blade of grass

in the yard, as various,
unfathomable.

Our first time together, fast
friends, for all the loving

your mother gave me, her care,
yours. I regret the time to come,

that we should live so far away,
that I will return to find you

sitting up, and then crawling,
walking from your mothers'

arms, saying my name
when I'm not there. What is it

a love like this—some vanity?
some reparation?—that wishes

you would not learn the world
without me.

The Summer

That no one mentioned when I came to meet you
        for a lake swim the afternoon after your wedding:
        don't mind the deer carcass at the corner
        of our driveway, don't mind the black
        cavern in its cheek, nor the small too-white
        stalactite bone of its jaw.

That I was grieving the mother of a friend who died
        after a slow death in hospice and the teenage
        daughter of others dead in a log cabin
        fire that same weekend.

That we celebrate our lives in contrast
        to these misfortunes for these misfortunes
        are not ours.

That we love our friends and that this love
        is hard to describe for it is slippery
        as lake water. Always steady and always
        changing, it tells us nothing of our future.

That we have a future. That your wedding
        is our promise as well.

That we ate spiced rabbit for dinner and talked
        about our friend who collapsed
        in the shower last summer.

That death is all
        around us, that the more people you love
        the more you have to bury.

That I'd been wondering if I should kiss
        a particular boy and if that counted
        as an old pattern I should break
        —success being the closest difference
        between romance and
        a habit one can't undo.

That a grasshopper snapped its wings over the yard.

That there were hot dogs and apple pie.

That we cried
        more during the ceremony
        than at the side of the road.

That that is how it should be, if we're lucky,
        and learn well to love
        what's coming and what's here.

That your cousin instructed us to return
        from the lake with something interesting and
        we didn't think of it again once the Frisbee arrived.

That so many of us write poems and worry
        for our health and well-being and none
        thought to mention the deer in advance.

That its leggy corpse was rock, more
      solid than resting, so outwardly still in the face
      of flies and what else.

That I chose when applying sunscreen
      to his broad-shouldered back
      to regard my hand
      as a third party
      so it would not betray me.

That death, when it came for her mother,
      was a blessing for my dutiful friend.

That deer were everywhere
      those summer nights, a portend
      for I knew not what. One hoof
      stepping off the curb.

Wolf Lake

It was down that road I brought her, still
in the trunk of my car. The late September
sun continued to burn, my skin slick
with sweat and dusted with the grit
of the road. In the back window, the drone
of a horsefly desperate to get out, wings small
dull chainsaws against the glass. I was eager
to be rid of the noise. There are sounds
I cannot forget. Her clucking as I carried her
over the brittle, yellow grass, steel against
wetted bone, our huffy breathing like lovers
after a vigorous dance. I say the apartment did it.
By the end of summer, I could hear everything
which living alone provides—the kitchen knives
asleep in the drawer, the sunken couch, even
the carpet lonely for something more than my
two dumb feet. Some moods are so black
they move backwards. We never loved
the campgrounds and lake, clear nights
passing a jay at the beach. Don't be fooled.
The world can be taken from us more easily
than we from it. I learned it's hard
to kill a girl. You've got to cut her deep
and you've got to cut her right and I had done
neither. Nothing about that night was easy.
I loved my Chrysler and knew there would
be blood. Unlocking the trunk, my guts roiled
for what was next. Months of thinking
came down to this, my future and my past
bound in the moment, waiting for release

to be its own pleasure. Hell yes, I've lived
to recognize the cage, each of us born to serve
desire, to suckle life and spit it up, hungry,
unsatisfied. Let's not be fools. Take all
you can. The crows on my back lawn
which made a sparrow a meal taught me
after death a girl is no less a girl, nor less
valuable. Animals, like God, love all things,
the living and the dead, equally. Only we
have a word for corpse. Still, you ask question
after question, struggling to uncover why,
which could be answered if you had any interest
in how. Her hands spooned like lovers tied
behind her back and her clothes sequined
with blood. Finally, she looked me in the eye
as a pickup rounded the corner and I knew
I would lose her. Her body wet and limp
over my shoulder as the truck fishtailed
to a stop. She was too much. I dropped her
and ran for the trees. The second shot
hit my shoulder and bone lodged in my eye.
I fell. I tasted what I thought must be
somebody else's blood, and the woods.

A New Song

Here in this narrow seat
with a god's eye view
from the belly of unfathomable
mechanics, 36,077 feet
from the earth, I want only to grace
the broad back of a man
each tender moment his arm
appears between his seat
and the wall.

               I am no fool.

I can pull this line
of desire until it yanks
free my father, who is ash

unsettling along the bed
of the St Lawrence
a short row from shore.

My comfortless Adam.

Years back, alive, his arms
were full, holding,
what—
         a brambled apology
impossible to set down.

Today I'm listening to music
on an airplane headed toward
home. I resist touching
a stranger. La Havas sings
We all make mistakes, we do.
I learned from you.

LITTLE THINGS

A Little Porno Story

Muscles clusterfuck
the slick skin of a young man

pale with fatigue.
A common midnight.

The scenario
belies simplicity:

cameramen, lights, fluffers,
catering, drugs

of a kind. Though
a dream of violence

will not contain itself,
we have no fear

in the hands of others.
We have been primed

for this, for submission
for so many of us

have been rejected
finally, we are relieved

to be owned. Wishing
is now equal to luck.

A Little Story of a Bad Idea

I retrieve
from under my father's
hospital bed a dollar
store bag holding one
final boot.

>   *He lost me*
>   *to a cocktail*

As he slumbers
on meds from his leg
amputation, I slit the toe

>   *of diabetes and drinking,*
>   *right, so I throw up*

of leather
            from its sole,
making the cut a mouth.

>   *gags about malt*
>   *and hops.*

Reposition the tongue.
Stitch pant leg to boot's
maw.

>   *I'm drunk*
>   *with power*

Two white buttons
on the black leather
form eyes, the puppet

>   *a step ahead*
>   *of your old man.*

of my father's leg
comes alive.

>   *(Ain't he*
>   *the heel.)*

He snips free
the right limbs

>   *the joker*
>   *who cuts you up.*

of my father's jeans, tosses them
to the trash beside
other shoes.

>   *Can't say*
>   *who animates me, baby*

He frees the final leg, folds
the denim neatly, and presents
the material to me

>   *my ass end's*
>   *an open wound.*

Everything is fucked.

his son imagining
too many things.

A Little Story of the Burden in the World

This afternoon in the dry hills a group
                    of writers gathered in a stucco
          bungalow to discuss your new poems.

Nancy says something about how the book
          is infected with names. Manorhamilton,
                    Gardom Lake, Bloodroot,
                              Moher, Hector, Homer.

What gives?
                    I'm thinking
back to our conversation the day before,
          how I build poems that
kaleidoscope a narrative, attempt nuances
          in turns of thought
                              along certain lines,

and you build by a pattern of details that
          when placed together
                              outline an inarticulable thing.

Imagine
                    buckets of paint
thrown towards an invisible giraffe.
That.

                    The other day a few of us writers
were joking about how we count things
          —tables in a room, floor tiles,
                    staccato highway lines. Bugs.
                              Not that knowing

will make life easier
but counting feels like a talisman for safety,
            a pebble in the hand fallen
    from the mountain of all we can't fathom.

So it strikes me these names aren't
            about the poem trying to know something
anew, not an insight, because even
                        the shadows of your galloping
                        children
        on a sunny day
                    are heavy with words.

Everything exists before them, your poems
            silently illustrate, so that only ignorance
                makes living possible.
Born into history,
                as their slim shoulders widen
they carry more of this
                    —do we say historical?—
burden
        of being alive.

Your poems are vandals, then, Sharon says,
            dismantling what pre-exists, robbing the rubble
                    to remake a point. Or to build a shelter,
                    maybe.
    At that moment her ginger
            poodle presents a prancing floppy
                    head, a moistened snout.
            I scratch its chest devotedly. I want this dog
    to like me because it too is innocent.

With my nails penetrating the tight curls
of a doggy beast whose name I have yet to know
I'm considering how just because
something begins
that doesn't make it new.
If you name a thing, you render it
less true.

A Little Rant for Whining

How do you critique without
the ignorant calling you
whiny?
      Maybe we title this poem
"Prayer for Whining," which, today,
is all about "A Prayer for Women
Who Tweet."
        #LeslieJones
Might as well include
prayer for women in the gaming industry,
in the paper, the pulpit, women
in comedy, in politics, women in film,
in uniform, in sports. Prayer
for women who write, prayer
for women over forty,
prayer for women on Tindr,
or any dating site.
        Hands up, yeah?

It's a wonder we aren't shouting
all the time. We should be amazed
our women friends aren't
shouting all the time. Hashtag
grateful. #sanity #sitdown-
hater-andchokeonit.

How can Twitter not be gendered
male if it permits that deluge
of sexist assaults? If we can't
ban those pricks because
of freedom of speech

what gender would you guess
our freedom to be?

What race?
          Okay okay
if we want to bitch
about bitching then let's
count how many words
we wrote on Facebook either critiquing
or defending Black Lives Matter

#intersectionality #sameoldshit
#blackpeoplearequeerpeople2
on repeat

and compare those numbers

to our word count on healing
or strategies. Hashtag remedies.

I thought so.

A Little Story of Dissociation

Concrete gives up its heat as dogs
of the neighbourhood rest
in the long grass behind the hall.
This evening offers the kind of breeze
        after a summer wedding a family needs
            to best enjoy the night, dancing.

They're neighbours in light linen dresses
        who call across the street
           to join them.
        Simply wave, pretending
    to have not heard right.
Return home.

        Sprawl on the couch,
log into a computer, use someone's
      password, chat in a chat room
        with someone else's name
    to arrange a stranger's
rendez-vous.

In the safety of someone's home someone
        leaves the front door unlocked,
      undresses, crawls into someone's bed
with sheets thrown accidentally
        on purpose across someone's
        exposed ass.

In the hall up the street the backs
of men and women are slick with effort
dancing to Motown. The floorboards
keep time with the walls.
Some other someone
here

lets himself in
to someone else's home, slides
a tongue in someone's crack,
slicks someone up and raw
ruts this someone's hole.
Someone
thinks he can hear through
a downstairs window all those shoes
hitting the hall floor
with a force of joy
or determination.

An evening is made
from thousands of unchoreographed
dramas. A party, a mania of heat,
dogs and cool breezes,
a whole host of someones
invited to dance.

A Little Story of Solace

The cruising beach
            presents a hummingbird, the dark
                        head of a seal rising
above water, a heron,
            four wasps in a log beside me
building their nest

If I can make a twig
                        snagging my clothing
            a sign
to go no further, how is it
                        I have no will
to end the hunt outside myself

                    We are here
        for our pitiable
        bodies
                    lush trails
        mock our fumbling, zippers
        and latex

            Maybe
        we are lonely
            for the world

to have silence, this silence
      here on the beach, the silence
            of grass
     torn from itself by the black beak
of a goose, silence in the lick
    of water, in birdcall,
          silence in the leaves

silence in this loneliness

loneliness
    in some muscle
       God's hand
that holds everything

     and lets go.

A Little Song to Make Sense of the World

After my father died my uncle
told me a story about

my father being abused
by a kid in their neighbourhood.

I need even more people
to die before I can tell

all I was told though
fuck it.

If information is a knife,
a story is the blanket

we wrap it in.
Give me a word—

I'm searching a word
for that moment when

a teenager was discovered
abusing a boy

who would be my father.
Something to articulate

whose hands
were where? How

nobody told us
the choices

we could make. This poem
a product

of choices nobody told us
we could make.

Is it sickness to be haunted
by your father's body?

I'm gambling if you study
a puzzle long enough

you may find peace
with finding no peace.

What tool is sharp enough
to dull all the things

you cannot do
about the past?

Four years later, I am still
imagining. Across

the table from me,
slicing apricots for a tarte tatin,

is the man I married
who my father never met.

What is a life that this
could be possible?

Some truths are so cutting
we need a story

to hold them. Hold them.
Hold them.

Notes

Some poems here borrow from others. Most notably, "Wolf Lake" is after Matt Rader's original poem by the same title, with Elizabeth Bachinsky's "Wolf Lake" second, and mine for a trio.

"A Little Story of Dissociation" found an echo from "A Beautiful Night for the Rodeo" by Keetje Kuipers. "Prayer for Envy" grew from Naomi Shihab Nye's "Famous." "Prayer for Happiness" is after both "Happiness" by Jane Kenyon and "Happiness" by Stephen Dunn. Many others grew from many others; apologies for any oversights my narrow memory produces.

"Prayer for a Family Friend" and "I Dream of Fraternity" were previously published in *Canadian Literature*.

"Prayer for Irony" and "Prayer for a Time of Change" appeared in *Matrix: 100 poems dossier*.

"I Dream the Inevitable" appeared in *Plenitude Magazine*.

"I Dream of Good Management" was previously titled "I Dreamt I was MCing" and appeared in *Fogged Clarity: An Arts Review*.

"Prayer for a New Song" appeared in *CV2*.

"Your Peers Die Like This" appeared in *Matrix*.

Versions of "Prayer for Promiscuity", "Prayer for Paternal Love", "Prayer for Solace," "Prayer for Renewal" and "Letter, 10:28pm" appeared in *Prism International*.

"Wolf Lake" previously appeared in *IV Lounge Nights*.

Acknowledgements

Thank you to each exceptional subconscious who provided material for the Dreams of Friends and Family a decade ago: Emily Schultz, Colin Thomas, Shauna Baitz, Flick Harrison, Brian Cartwright and Diego Maranan. I edited each a little, sometimes adding details here and there, but mostly they appear intact.

My deep thanks to readers of these poems, who offered great advice and feedback over the years: Bronwyn Berg, Matt Rader, Cole Mash, Colin Thomas, Francis Langevin and the tireless magazine editors who've previously published this work. Thanks to the Faculty of Creative and Critical Studies at UBC Okanagan campus, who employ me in a profession I adore.

Most of this book was written on the unceded territory of the Syilx (Okanagan) Peoples. I'm deeply grateful to this place, in part for the wonder it inspires in me and for the security I have felt on this land.

Thanks to Amber McMillan for giving these poems such a careful read. Every suggestion was a pleasure. Thanks to Michael Caines for the use his amazing painting as the cover of this book. Thanks to the crew at Nightwood for making a beautiful book. And great thanks to Silas White for welcoming me in. It's thrilling to be counted amongst so many poets and books I admire.

About the Author

Michael V. Smith is a writer, comedian, filmmaker, performance artist and occasional clown. He is the author of several books including *What You Can't Have* (Signature, 2006), which was shortlisted for the ReLit Award, and *My Body Is Yours* (Arsenal Pulp, 2015), which was a Lambda Literary Award finalist. He is also the winner of the inaugural Dayne Ogilvie Prize for LGBT Emerging Writers and was nominated for the Journey Prize. Smith currently teaches creative writing at the University of British Columbia's Okanagan campus in Kelowna. *Bad Ideas* is his latest collection of poetry.

Photo Credit: Lise Guyot (L.G. Photography)